ANNE GEDDES®

little blessings

sourcebooks

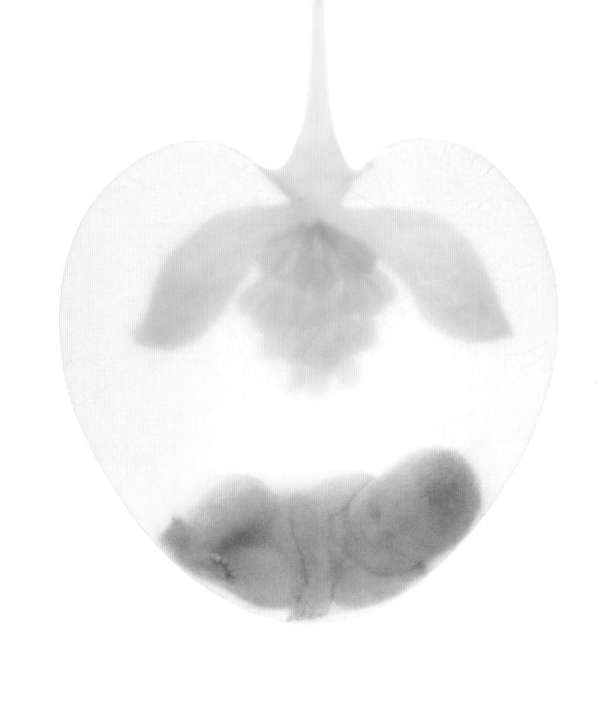

Sometimes the
only blessing you
need to count is
a heartbeat.

Making the decision
to have a child—it's
momentous. It is to
decide forever to have
your heart go walking
outside your body.

—*Elizabeth Stone*

The largest of
blessings are those
that are small.

There is no other closeness in human life like the closeness between a mother and her baby—chronologically, physically, and spiritually they are just a few heartbeats away from being the same person.

—Susan Chever

The moment a child is born, a mother is also born. The woman existed, but the mother, never. The mother is something absolutely new.

—Rajneesh

Sometimes when you pick up your child you can feel the map of your own bones beneath your hands, or smell the scent of your skin in the nape of his neck. This is the most extraordinary thing about motherhood—finding a piece of yourself separate and apart…

—*Jodi Picoult*

Dear Child,

You are the poem
I dreamed of writing,
The masterpiece
I longed to paint.

You are the shining star
I reached for in my ever-hopeful quest
For life fulfilled…

You are my child.

Now with all things
I am blessed.

A baby is born
with a need to be
loved, and never
outgrows it.

—Frank A. Clark

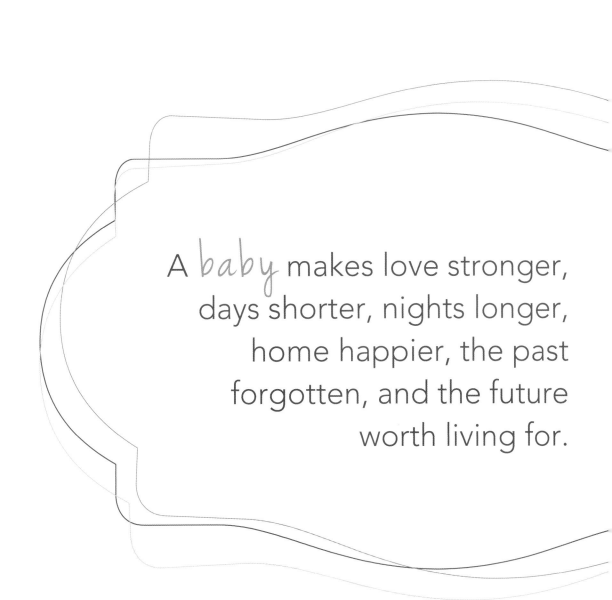

A *baby* makes love stronger, days shorter, nights longer, home happier, the past forgotten, and the future worth living for.

May your day be filled with blessings, like the sun that lights the sky, and may you have the courage to spread your wings and fly.

Blessed is
the influence
of one true
loving human
soul on
another.

—*George Eliot*

Celtic Blessing

May the strength of the wind and the light of the sun,

The softness of the rain and the mystery of the moon

Reach you and fill you.

May beauty delight you and happiness uplift you,

May wonder fulfill you and love surround you.

May your step be steady and your arm be strong,

May your heart be peaceful and your word be true.

May you seek to learn, may you learn to live,

May you live to love, and may you love—always.

When I count
        my blessings,
I count you twice.

Having a place to go is home.
Having someone to love is family.
Having both is a blessing.

Jewish Blessing

In every birth, blessed is the wonder.

In every creation, blessed is the new beginning.

In every child, blessed is life.

In every hope, blessed is the potential.

In every transition, blessed is the beginning.

In every existence, blessed are the possibilities.

In every love, blessed are the tears.

In every life, blessed is the love.

There are three names by which a person is called:

One which her father and mother call her,

And one which people call her,

And one which she earns for herself.

The best one of these is the one that she earns for herself.

Some people dream of angels. I hold one in my arms.

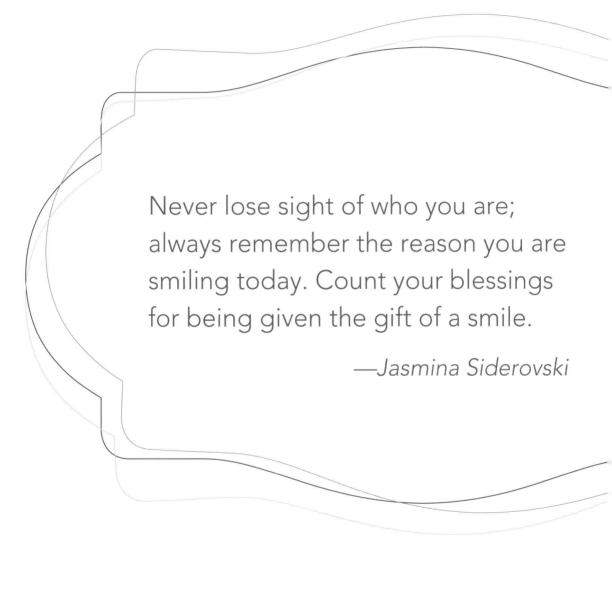

Never lose sight of who you are; always remember the reason you are smiling today. Count your blessings for being given the gift of a smile.

—*Jasmina Siderovski*

When the first baby laughed for the first time,
the laugh broke into
a thousand pieces
and they all went skipping about,
and that was the beginning of fairies.
And now when every new baby is born its
first laugh becomes a fairy. So there ought to be
one fairy for every boy or girl.

—James Matthew Barrie

No one can fully imagine a life with children. After they are born, no one can ever imagine a life without them.

First we had each other,
then we had you,
now we have everything.

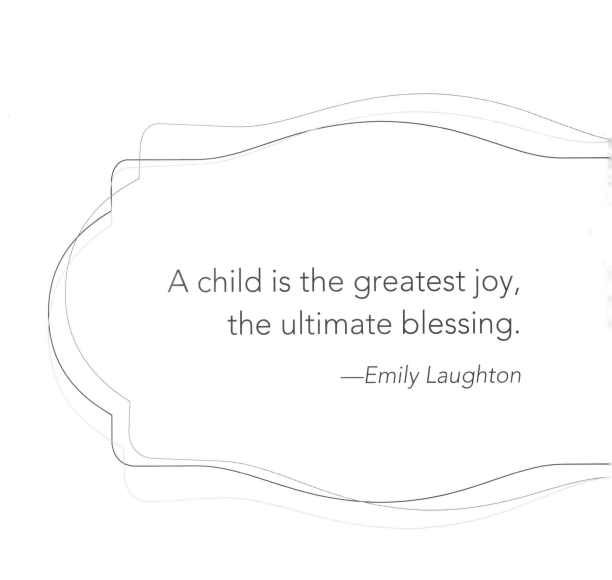

A child is the greatest joy,
the ultimate blessing.

—*Emily Laughton*

Not what
we say
about our
blessings,
but how we
use them,
is the true
measure
of our
thanksgiving.

—*W. T. Purkiser*

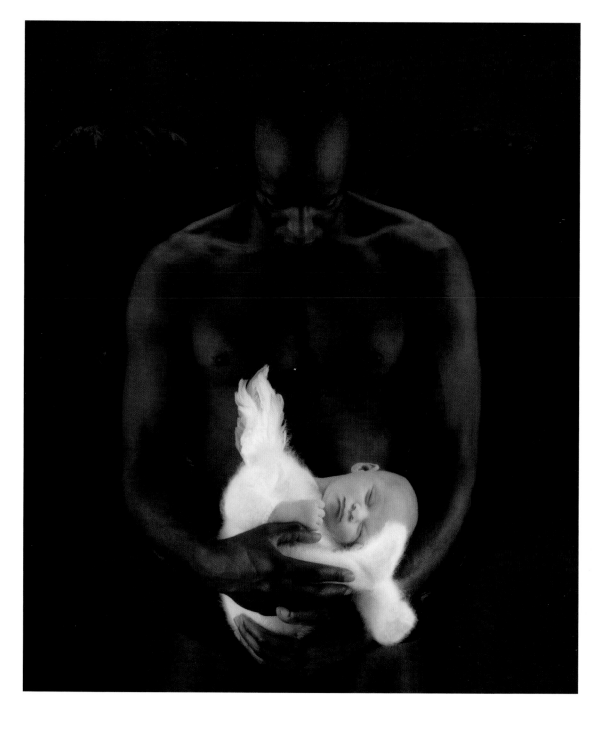

The soul is healed by being with children.

—Proverb

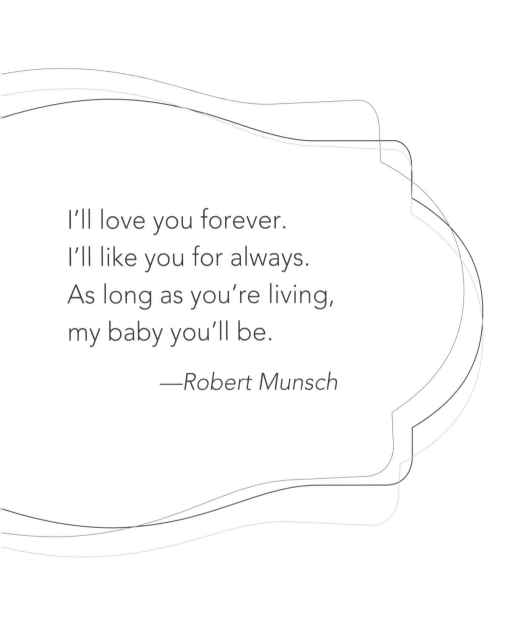

I'll love you forever.
I'll like you for always.
As long as you're living,
my baby you'll be.

—*Robert Munsch*

You are a child of
the universe, no
less than the trees
and the stars.

—Desiderata

From the Tao Te Ching

Giving birth and nourishing,

having without possessing,

acting with no expectations,

leading and not trying to control:

this is the supreme virtue.

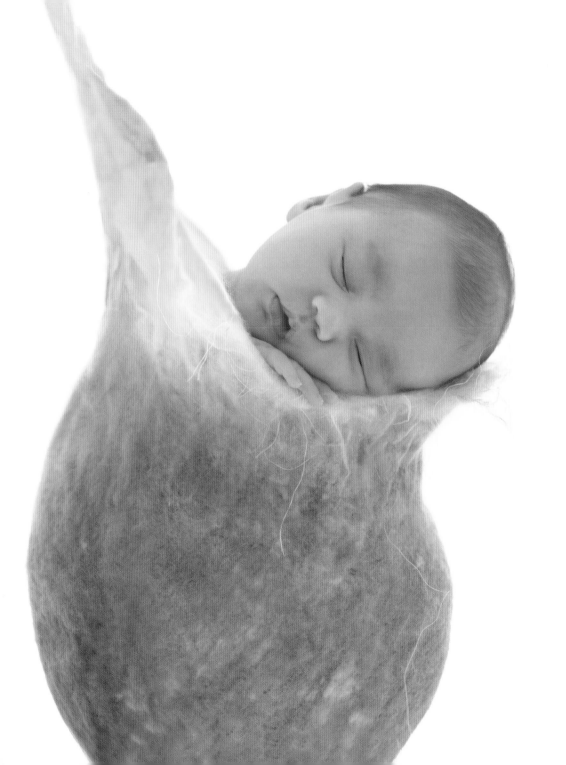

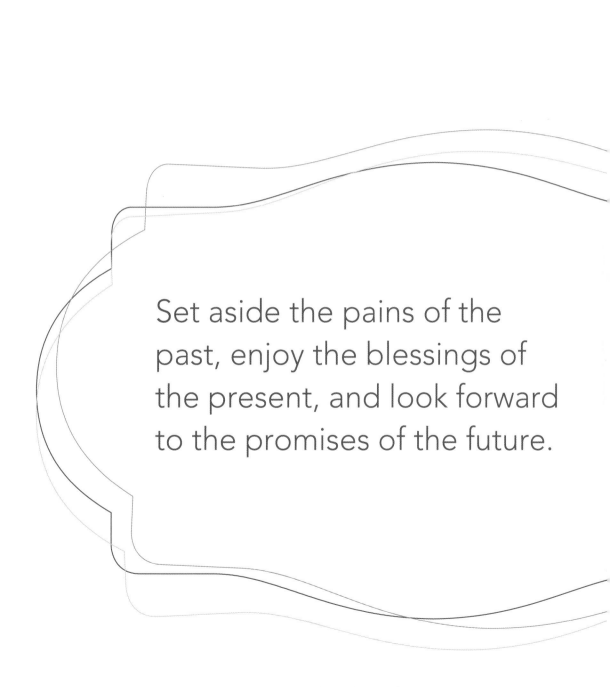

Set aside the pains of the past, enjoy the blessings of the present, and look forward to the promises of the future.

There are two ways to live your life. One is as though nothing is a miracle. The other is as though everything is a miracle.

—Albert Einstein

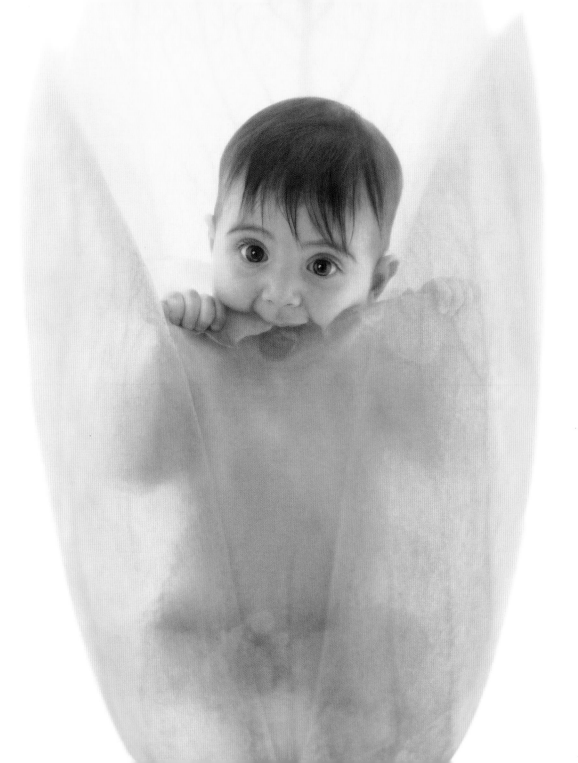

A new baby is like the beginning of all things—wonder, hope, and a dream of possibilities.

—Eda LeShan

Write your
troubles in the
sand. Carve
your blessings
in stone.

We should certainly

count our blessings,

but we should also

make our blessings count.

—Neal A. Maxwell.

Sourcebooks and the colophon are registered trademarks of Sourcebooks, Inc.

Published by Sourcebooks, Inc.
(630) 961-3900
Fax: (630) 961-2168
www.sourcebooks.com

Library of Congress Cataloging-in-Publication data is on file with the publisher.

Printed and bound in the China.
LEO 10 9 8 7 6 5 4 3 2 1